BREAKING

A GUIDE TO ESCAPING TOXIC R

BY

ANTHONY RUSSO

2023

Breaking Free: A Guide to Escaping Toxic Relationships by Anthony Russo
This edition was created and published by Mamba Press
©MambaPress 2023

Contents

Preface

In the intricate and often bewildering realm of human relationships, there exists a dark side that can hold us captive, draining us of our vitality and spirit. This book, "Breaking Free: A Guide to Escaping Toxic Relationships," emerges as a source of solace and guidance for those who have felt the suffocating grip of such relationships. Within these pages, we embark on a journey of discovery, recovery, and transformation, illuminating the path towards emancipation from the clutches of toxicity.

The bonds that tie us to toxic relationships, whether they be romantic entanglements, friendships, family dynamics, or professional alliances, can be profoundly destructive. They corrode our self-esteem, obscure our self-worth, and, at times, even threaten our very existence. Yet, within this darkness, there is hope—a beacon that guides us towards the light of healing and personal liberation.

This book unfolds as a heartfelt response to the countless individuals who have experienced the anguish of toxic relationships. It offers an understanding of what characterizes such relationships, the warning signs that should not be ignored, and the emotional toll they can exact. Furthermore, "Breaking Free" furnishes you with a comprehensive roadmap—a blueprint to reclaim your autonomy, rebuild your self-esteem, and cultivate healthier relationships.

Throughout the ensuing chapters, we will embark on a journey of self-discovery, learning, and empowerment. We will explore the roots of toxic relationships, delve into the intricacies of self-reflection, discuss the essentiality of forging a support system, and delve into the art of setting and maintaining boundaries. We will lay out the crucial steps to planning your escape from toxicity, provide guidance on navigating the inevitable emotional challenges, and offer insights on the path of healing and renewal.

As you turn these pages, remember that you are not alone. Countless individuals have faced similar trials and tribulations, and many have successfully emerged from the shadows of toxic relationships, emerging stronger, wiser, and more resilient. This book is here to accompany you on your journey, offering insights, strategies, and stories of triumph that will empower you to embark on your own path towards breaking free from toxicity. Your life can be filled with healthier, more nurturing relationships, and it all begins with the courage to take the first step.

Introduction

In the intricate tapestry of human relationships, the threads that bind us are as diverse as the people themselves. Some connections bring us joy, laughter, and support, while others challenge us to grow and evolve. Yet, within this mosaic of human interactions, there exists a shadowy corner—an abyss where the bonds that tie us become chains, and the relationships that were meant to nurture our souls instead drain us of our vitality. These are the toxic relationships that haunt our lives, leaving scars both seen and unseen.

This book, "Breaking Free: A Guide to Escaping Toxic Relationships," is a lifeline for those who find themselves ensnared in such harmful connections. Within these pages, we embark on a journey—a journey that begins with recognizing the signs of toxicity, leads us through the labyrinth of emotions that accompany these relationships, and ultimately guides us toward the path of healing and liberation.

A toxic relationship is like a poison that slowly seeps into your life, affecting your mental, emotional, and sometimes even physical well-being. It can manifest in various forms: a romantic partnership that leaves you feeling trapped and powerless, a friendship that saps your energy and self-esteem, a family dynamic that is suffocating, or a workplace relationship that erodes your sense of self-worth. Toxicity can wear many masks, but it always leaves behind a trail of destruction.

In these pages, we will shine a light on the darkness of toxic relationships. We will explore what defines such relationships, the common patterns and behaviors that characterize them, and the insidious emotional toll they take on individuals. By recognizing the signs of toxicity, you are taking the first step towards breaking free.

However, breaking free is not a simple task. It is a journey that requires courage, self-reflection, and resilience. It is a journey that often requires the support of friends, family, or professionals. It is a journey that demands the establishment and maintenance of healthy boundaries. It is a journey that necessitates careful planning and emotional fortitude.

Yet, it is also a journey that promises healing, renewal, and the opportunity to rebuild your life on your terms. It is a journey that holds the promise of rediscovering your self-worth, nurturing healthier relationships, and ultimately finding the happiness and peace you deserve.

As we embark on this journey together, remember that you are not alone. Many have walked this path before you, and many have emerged on the other side, stronger and more empowered than ever. "Breaking Free" is here to guide you, to provide you with insights, strategies, and the strength to take that first step towards a life free from toxicity. Your journey begins now, and with each page you turn, you move one step closer to breaking free and reclaiming your life.

Recognizing Toxicity

In the intricate dance of human relationships, it can be challenging to recognize when a connection has turned toxic. We often cling to the hope that things will improve, that the person causing us harm will change, or that we can endure the pain just a little longer. But there comes a time when we must face the truth: we are in a toxic relationship, and it's imperative to acknowledge it.

Identifying Toxic Relationships

To begin your journey toward freedom, you must first understand what constitutes a toxic relationship. Toxic relationships are characterized by patterns of behavior that undermine your well-being, self-esteem, and happiness. These patterns often include:

1. **Constant Criticism:** In a toxic relationship, criticism is relentless. Your partner, friend, or family member may find fault in everything you do, eroding your self-esteem and self-worth.
2. **Control and Manipulation:** Toxic individuals often seek to control your actions, thoughts, and decisions. They may use manipulation tactics, such as guilt-tripping or gaslighting, to maintain dominance.
3. **Emotional Abuse:** Emotional abuse can take many forms, including insults, humiliation, and threats. It leaves deep emotional scars and can shatter your self-confidence.
4. **Isolation:** Toxic individuals may isolate you from friends and family, making you more dependent on them. This isolation can be a powerful tool for maintaining control.
5. **Inconsistency:** Toxic relationships are marked by inconsistency. One moment, the person may be loving and supportive, and the next, they may become hostile and hurtful. This unpredictability keeps you off-balance.

6. **Lack of Empathy:** Toxic individuals often lack empathy and compassion. They may disregard your feelings and needs, focusing solely on their own desires.

7. **Excessive Drama:** Toxic relationships are often riddled with drama and conflict. The constant turmoil can be exhausting and damaging to your emotional well-being.

Recognizing the Warning Signs

Recognizing a toxic relationship requires a keen awareness of the warning signs. Some of these signs may include:

- **Feeling Drained:** If spending time with someone consistently leaves you feeling emotionally drained or physically exhausted, it may be a sign of toxicity.
- **Loss of Self-Identity:** In a toxic relationship, you may begin to lose your sense of self. Your interests, desires, and aspirations become secondary to the demands of the toxic person.
- **Denial and Rationalization:** It's common to deny or rationalize the toxicity in a relationship. You might make excuses for the person's behavior or convince yourself that things will get better.
- **Isolation from Support:** Toxic individuals often isolate their victims from friends and family. If you find yourself becoming increasingly isolated, it's a red flag.
- **Physical Symptoms:** The stress and emotional turmoil of a toxic relationship can manifest as physical symptoms such as headaches, digestive problems, or sleep disturbances.

The Power of Acknowledgment

Acknowledging that you are in a toxic relationship is the first step towards breaking free. It can be a difficult and painful realization, but it is also a powerful one. It is the moment when you take control of your narrative and decide that you deserve better.

In the chapters ahead, we will delve deeper into the complexities of toxic relationships and guide you on the path to breaking free. Remember, you are not alone on this journey, and there is hope for a brighter, healthier future beyond toxicity.

Self-Reflection and Acceptance

Having recognized the toxicity within your relationship, you've taken the courageous first step toward liberation. Now, it's time to embark on a journey of self-reflection and self-acceptance. This chapter will guide you in understanding your role in the toxic dynamic and embracing self-acceptance as the cornerstone of your path to freedom.

Understanding Your Role

Toxic relationships are seldom one-sided. Understanding your role within the dynamic is crucial to breaking free. Consider the following aspects:

1. **Boundaries:** Reflect on your boundaries and whether they were too porous or rigid. Did you allow the toxic person to overstep your limits, or did you consistently push them away?
2. **Self-Esteem:** Assess your self-esteem. Did you enter the relationship with a healthy sense of self-worth, or did your self-esteem suffer as a result of the toxicity?
3. **Communication:** Evaluate your communication patterns. Did you assert your needs and concerns effectively, or did you withdraw or become passive-aggressive?
4. **Expectations:** Examine your expectations of the relationship. Were they realistic, or did you cling to unrealistic hopes of change or improvement?
5. **Patterns from the Past:** Reflect on whether the toxic relationship mirrors patterns from your past, such as family dynamics or previous relationships.
6. **Coping Mechanisms:** Consider how you coped with the stress of the toxic relationship. Did you resort to unhealthy coping mechanisms, such as substance abuse or self-isolation?

Embracing Self-Acceptance

Self-acceptance is the foundation upon which you will rebuild your life and relationships. It is the unwavering belief that you are worthy of love, respect, and happiness, just as you are. Here's how to nurture self-acceptance:

1. **Practice Self-Compassion:** Treat yourself with the same kindness and understanding you would offer a dear friend. Self-compassion allows you to acknowledge your imperfections without judgment.
2. **Challenge Negative Self-Talk:** Replace self-criticism with self-affirmation. When you catch yourself engaging in negative self-talk, consciously redirect your thoughts toward self-empowerment.
3. **Seek Professional Help:** If your self-esteem is deeply wounded, consider therapy or counseling. A qualified therapist can guide you through the process of healing and self-discovery.
4. **Surround Yourself with Positivity:** Surround yourself with supportive friends and family who affirm your worth. Cultivate relationships that celebrate your strengths and encourage your growth.
5. **Set Realistic Expectations:** Understand that no one is perfect, including yourself. Set achievable goals and expectations for your personal growth and the relationships you want to cultivate.
6. **Journaling:** Keep a journal to record your thoughts, feelings, and progress. Journaling can be a powerful tool for self-reflection and self-expression.

The Power of Self-Acceptance

Self-acceptance is your shield against future toxic relationships. When you fully embrace your worth, you become less susceptible to manipulation and mistreatment. Your boundaries become firmer, your self-esteem soars, and your capacity for healthier relationships expands.

Remember, the journey toward self-acceptance is ongoing. It's not about striving for perfection but learning to love and accept yourself in all your beautifully imperfect ways. As you continue on this path, you'll find the strength and resilience to break free from toxic relationships and build a life filled with love, respect, and genuine connections.

Building a Support System

In your quest to break free from a toxic relationship, one of the most critical assets you can cultivate is a strong support system. This chapter explores the importance of building and nurturing a network of friends, family, and professionals who can provide you with guidance, understanding, and a safe haven during challenging times.

The Role of Support in Recovery

Toxic relationships often leave individuals feeling isolated and emotionally drained. Building a support system is essential for several reasons:

1. **Validation:** A support system can validate your experiences and feelings, assuring you that what you're going through is real and significant.
2. **Emotional Release:** Sharing your thoughts and emotions with supportive individuals can serve as a therapeutic release, alleviating stress and anxiety.
3. **Perspective:** Trusted friends, family members, or therapists can offer valuable perspectives and insights, helping you see the situation more clearly.
4. **Strength and Resilience:** Knowing that you have a safety net of support can empower you to take difficult steps toward breaking free from the toxic relationship.

Identifying Your Support Network

Your support network may include different types of individuals, each playing a unique role:

1. **Friends:** Close friends who understand your situation and offer emotional support are invaluable. Lean on those you trust the most.

2. **Family:** Family members who are supportive and understanding can provide a sense of security and belonging.
3. **Support Groups:** Consider joining support groups or online communities where you can connect with others who have experienced or are experiencing toxic relationships.
4. **Therapists or Counselors:** Professional help can be a lifeline. Therapists or counselors can offer guidance, coping strategies, and a safe space for discussing your experiences.
5. **Mentors or Role Models:** Seek out individuals who have successfully navigated toxic relationships or faced similar challenges. Their wisdom and insights can be invaluable.
6. **Legal and Financial Advisors:** In cases of extreme toxicity, legal or financial professionals may be necessary to help you protect your rights and assets.

Nurturing Your Support System

Building a support system is an ongoing process that requires effort and care. Here's how to nurture your support network:

1. **Open Communication:** Keep the lines of communication with your support network open. Share your thoughts and feelings honestly, and encourage them to do the same.
2. **Boundaries:** Set boundaries within your support system to ensure that your needs are met without overwhelming any single individual.
3. **Gratitude:** Express gratitude to those who support you. Acknowledging their contributions can strengthen your relationships.
4. **Reciprocity:** Be willing to offer support in return when your loved ones need it. A healthy support system is built on mutual care and respect.
5. **Professional Guidance:** Consider seeking professional help, such as therapy or counseling, to supplement your support

network. A therapist can offer specialized guidance and coping strategies.

The Power of Support

In the journey to break free from toxicity, your support system can be your lifeline. It's a reminder that you are not alone, that people care about your well-being, and that you have the strength to overcome adversity. As you continue on this path, remember that building and nurturing your support system is an essential step toward healing and reclaiming your life.

Setting Boundaries

Setting and maintaining healthy boundaries is a pivotal step in your journey to break free from a toxic relationship. This chapter explores the importance of boundaries, how to establish them, and why they are essential for your well-being.

The Importance of Boundaries

Boundaries are like the fences around your emotional and physical space. In a toxic relationship, these fences may have been trampled upon or ignored, leading to emotional harm and distress. Here's why boundaries are crucial:

1. **Protection:** Boundaries protect your emotional, mental, and physical well-being. They define what is acceptable and unacceptable behavior in your relationships.
2. **Self-Respect:** Setting boundaries is an act of self-respect. It communicates to others that you value yourself and your needs.
3. **Clarity:** Boundaries provide clarity in your relationships. They set expectations and reduce misunderstandings.
4. **Autonomy:** Healthy boundaries allow you to maintain your autonomy and make decisions that align with your values and desires.

Types of Boundaries

Boundaries can be categorized into several types:

1. **Physical Boundaries:** These define your personal space and physical comfort level. They include rules about physical touch and personal belongings.
2. **Emotional Boundaries:** Emotional boundaries govern your feelings, allowing you to protect yourself from emotional

manipulation or abuse.

3. **Mental Boundaries:** These relate to your thoughts and beliefs. Mental boundaries involve respecting each other's opinions and not trying to control or invalidate them.

4. **Time Boundaries:** Setting limits on your time and availability is essential. It ensures you have time for self-care and other important aspects of your life.

Establishing Boundaries

Here are steps to help you establish healthy boundaries:

1. **Self-Awareness:** Reflect on your needs, values, and what makes you comfortable or uncomfortable in relationships. Understanding yourself is key to setting effective boundaries.

2. **Communicate Clearly:** Express your boundaries in a clear and assertive manner. Use "I" statements to communicate how you feel and what you need.

3. **Be Consistent:** Consistency is vital. Enforce your boundaries consistently, even when it's challenging or uncomfortable.

4. **Practice Self-Care:** Taking care of your physical and emotional well-being strengthens your ability to maintain boundaries.

5. **Seek Support:** Discuss your boundaries with your support system, such as friends, family, or a therapist. They can provide guidance and encouragement.

Challenges in Boundary Setting

Setting boundaries can be challenging, especially in toxic relationships where the other person may resist or react negatively. Here are some common challenges:

1. **Guilt:** You may feel guilty for asserting your boundaries, especially if the toxic person tries to manipulate you with guilt.

2. **Fear of Consequences:** There may be fear of retaliation or negative consequences when you set boundaries.
3. **Emotional Attachments:** Emotional attachments can make it difficult to enforce boundaries with someone you care about deeply.
4. **Self-Doubt:** Toxic individuals may try to undermine your confidence in your boundaries. Stay true to your needs and values.

The Empowerment of Boundaries

As you work on setting and maintaining boundaries, remember that boundaries are an act of self-love and self-respect. They empower you to create healthier relationships and protect your well-being. While it may be challenging, the journey to establish and enforce boundaries is a transformative one, leading you closer to freedom from toxicity and towards a life filled with respect and self-worth.

Planning Your Exit

Having recognized the toxicity in your relationship, reflected on your role, and established healthy boundaries, you've laid the groundwork for your journey to liberation. Now, it's time to carefully plan your exit from the toxic relationship. This chapter explores the steps to take, the resources to gather, and the strategies to employ as you prepare to break free.

Assess Your Safety

Before taking any steps, it's crucial to assess your safety. In some cases, toxic relationships can turn dangerous, and your well-being may be at risk. If you believe your safety is in jeopardy, consider these precautions:

1. **Create a Safety Plan:** Develop a safety plan that includes strategies for leaving safely, such as identifying a safe place to go and people you can turn to for support.
2. **Document Evidence:** If you've experienced physical or emotional abuse, document evidence, such as texts, emails, or photos. This documentation can be valuable if you need legal protection.
3. **Seek Professional Help:** Reach out to domestic violence shelters, hotlines, or local organizations that can provide support and guidance in leaving a dangerous situation.

Financial Preparation

Financial independence can be a significant factor in your ability to leave a toxic relationship. Here's how to prepare financially:

1. **Create a Budget:** Evaluate your financial situation and create a budget to understand your income, expenses, and potential savings.
2. **Establish Financial Independence:** If you share financial

accounts with the toxic person, work towards separating your finances and establishing financial independence.

3. **Save for Emergency Expenses:** Set aside money for emergency expenses that may arise during your transition.
4. **Explore Legal Options:** If you're married or have shared assets, consult with an attorney to understand your legal rights and options.

Secure a Support Network

Lean on your support system as you plan your exit. Inform trusted friends and family members about your decision and your timeline. Having emotional support during this process is invaluable.

Housing and Logistics

Consider the practical aspects of leaving:

1. **Secure Housing:** Determine where you will go after leaving. This could be with friends, family, or a safe shelter. Ensure your housing arrangements are secure before making your move.
2. **Logistics:** Plan the logistics of your departure, including transportation and the items you'll need to take with you.

Emotional Preparation

Leaving a toxic relationship can be emotionally challenging. Prepare yourself by:

1. **Seeking Therapy:** Consider therapy or counseling to address the emotional toll of leaving and to build coping strategies.
2. **Self-Care:** Prioritize self-care to manage stress and anxiety. Engage in activities that bring you comfort and relaxation.
3. **Positive Affirmations:** Practice positive affirmations to boost your self-esteem and confidence.

The Exit Strategy

When the time comes to exit the toxic relationship, execute your plan with care:

1. **Choose the Right Moment:** Timing can be crucial. Pick a moment when the toxic person is less likely to react explosively.
2. **Stay Firm:** Expect resistance and emotional manipulation. Stay firm in your decision and your boundaries.
3. **Limit Contact:** After leaving, limit contact with the toxic person. Block communication if necessary to protect your emotional well-being.

Seek Legal and Protective Measures

If you're facing legal or safety concerns, consider seeking legal protection, such as restraining orders or legal custody arrangements.

Post-Exit Support

After leaving, lean on your support system for emotional support and guidance. Continue therapy or counseling to aid in your healing process.

The Liberation Begins

Planning your exit from a toxic relationship is a monumental step toward your liberation. It signifies your courage, self-respect, and commitment to a healthier, happier future. While the journey may have its challenges, remember that you are not alone, and there is hope on the other side of toxicity. The path to healing and reclaiming your life begins with this courageous step.

Navigating Emotional Challenges

Leaving a toxic relationship is a significant and courageous step, but it is not without its emotional challenges. In this chapter, we will explore the rollercoaster of emotions you may experience during and after the process and provide strategies to help you navigate these emotional challenges with resilience and self-compassion.

The Emotional Rollercoaster

Leaving a toxic relationship can trigger a wide range of emotions, and these feelings may come in waves. It's essential to recognize that this emotional journey is a normal part of the healing process. Here are some of the emotions you may encounter:

1. **Grief:** You may grieve the loss of the relationship, even if it was toxic. This grief is valid, and it's essential to allow yourself to feel it.
2. **Relief:** You might experience a sense of relief and freedom after leaving the toxicity behind. This relief can coexist with grief.
3. **Anger:** Feelings of anger, resentment, and betrayal are common. These emotions may be directed toward the toxic person or yourself for staying in the relationship.
4. **Sadness:** Sadness is a natural response to the end of any relationship. It's important to acknowledge and process this sadness.
5. **Anxiety:** Leaving a toxic relationship can be anxiety-inducing as you navigate uncertainty and change.
6. **Loneliness:** You may feel lonely and isolated, especially if the toxic person was a significant part of your life.

Strategies for Navigating Emotional Challenges

1. **Self-Compassion:** Be gentle with yourself. Understand that it's normal to have a range of emotions. Practice self-compassion and self-kindness during this time.
2. **Therapy or Counseling:** Continue therapy or counseling to work through your emotions and develop coping strategies. A professional can provide guidance tailored to your specific needs.
3. **Support System:** Lean on your support system for emotional support. Share your feelings with trusted friends and family members who can offer empathy and understanding.
4. **Journaling:** Keeping a journal can be a therapeutic way to process your emotions. Write down your thoughts and feelings as a way of releasing them.
5. **Mindfulness and Meditation:** Mindfulness practices and meditation can help you stay grounded and manage overwhelming emotions.
6. **Seek Professional Help:** If your emotions become overwhelming or interfere with your daily life, consider seeking the support of a mental health professional who specializes in trauma or post-traumatic stress.
7. **Self-Care:** Prioritize self-care activities that bring you comfort and relaxation. This can include exercise, meditation, reading, or spending time in nature.
8. **Boundaries:** Continue to maintain healthy boundaries with the toxic person to protect your emotional well-being.

Coping with Triggers

Certain situations, places, or people may trigger memories or emotions related to the toxic relationship. It's essential to develop strategies for coping with these triggers:

1. **Identify Triggers:** Recognize what triggers your emotional responses. Awareness is the first step in managing triggers

effectively.

2. **Create a Safe Space:** Identify safe spaces or environments where you can retreat to when triggered.

3. **Grounding Techniques:** Practice grounding techniques, such as deep breathing or focusing on your senses, to stay present when triggered.

4. **Distraction:** Engage in distracting activities when needed, such as listening to music, drawing, or doing a puzzle.

Remember Your Progress

As you navigate these emotional challenges, remember to acknowledge your progress. Celebrate your strength and resilience for taking the steps to break free from toxicity. Healing takes time, but with self-compassion and the support of those who care about you, you can emerge from this emotional journey stronger and more empowered.

Healing and Moving Forward

Having embarked on the journey to break free from a toxic relationship, navigated emotional challenges, and established healthier boundaries, it's time to focus on healing and moving forward. In this final chapter, we explore the process of healing, self-discovery, and rebuilding your life with newfound strength and confidence.

The Healing Process

Healing is not a linear path; it's a dynamic and personal journey. Embrace the following principles as you move through this process:

1. **Self-Care:** Prioritize self-care as a daily practice. It includes nourishing your body, mind, and soul with activities that promote well-being and self-love.
2. **Patience:** Be patient with yourself. Healing takes time, and there will be setbacks along the way. Allow yourself to feel and process your emotions.
3. **Forgiveness:** Consider forgiveness as a means of releasing the emotional weight that comes with holding onto resentment. This does not mean condoning the toxic behavior but letting go for your own peace.
4. **Therapy or Counseling:** Continue therapy or counseling to address any lingering emotional wounds and work on personal growth.

Reconnecting with Yourself

Leaving a toxic relationship provides an opportunity to rediscover who you are. Use this time for self-discovery:

1. **Reflect on Your Values:** Reevaluate your values, goals, and priorities. What truly matters to you? What do you want to focus on in your life moving forward?

2. **Set New Goals:** Set new, achievable goals that align with your values. These goals can give you a sense of purpose and direction.

3. **Explore Interests:** Reconnect with old interests and explore new ones. Engaging in hobbies and passions can be therapeutic and fulfilling.

4. **Rebuild Self-Esteem:** Work on rebuilding your self-esteem. Challenge negative self-beliefs and focus on your strengths and accomplishments.

Cultivating Healthy Relationships

As you heal and move forward, you may be open to forming new, healthier relationships:

1. **Boundaries:** Continue to enforce and maintain healthy boundaries in all your relationships. These boundaries protect your well-being.

2. **Communication:** Practice open and honest communication with others. Express your needs and expectations clearly and respectfully.

3. **Red Flags:** Be aware of red flags in new relationships. Trust your instincts and prioritize your safety and well-being.

4. **Seek Support:** Lean on your support system when forming new relationships. Friends and family can offer valuable insights and guidance.

Maintaining Self-Care

Self-care should remain a constant practice in your life, even as you move forward. It is the foundation of your well-being and resilience. Remember that self-care is not selfish; it is an essential part of living a balanced and healthy life.

Final Thoughts

Breaking free from a toxic relationship is a remarkable achievement, a testament to your strength and resilience. As you embark on the journey of healing and moving forward, know that there is a world of opportunity, growth, and happiness waiting for you. While the scars of the past may remain, they serve as a testament to your courage and your capacity for transformation.

Ultimately, the story of your life is still being written, and you have the power to shape it into a narrative filled with love, self-acceptance, and authentic connections. The road ahead may have challenges, but it is also filled with possibilities and the promise of a brighter, healthier, and more fulfilling future. You are not defined by your past; you are defined by the strength and resilience with which you rise above it.

Conclusion

In the pages of "Breaking Free: A Guide to Escaping Toxic Relationships," we've embarked on a transformative journey—a journey that begins with recognition and ends with liberation. This journey is not just a path away from toxicity; it is a path toward self-discovery, healing, and empowerment.

Recognizing toxicity in your relationships was the first courageous step you took. It required a willingness to confront uncomfortable truths, to face the emotional turmoil, and to acknowledge that change was necessary. From there, you delved into the depths of self-reflection and self-acceptance, understanding that your own boundaries, self-esteem, and choices played pivotal roles in the dynamics of your relationships.

With the support of a network of caring individuals, you laid the groundwork for your escape. You planned your exit with meticulous care, taking into account your safety, your financial independence, and the emotional toll of leaving behind what was familiar, albeit toxic. You navigated the rollercoaster of emotions, acknowledging the grief, anger, and sadness, but also the relief and newfound freedom.

As you broke free, you discovered the power of setting boundaries, of clearly defining what you would and would not accept in your life. You established a support system that became your lifeline during challenging times. You learned to cope with triggers and manage the emotional challenges that came your way.

And finally, you entered the chapter of healing and moving forward—a chapter of self-care, self-discovery, and the cultivation of healthier relationships. You reconnected with your true self, set new goals, and embarked on a journey of self-compassion and self-love.

Remember that healing is not a destination; it is a lifelong journey. The scars of your past may remain, but they serve as a testament to your resilience and growth. As you move forward, know that you are not alone. Your support system, the insights gained from your experiences, and the strength you've discovered within yourself will guide you toward a brighter and more fulfilling future.

You have reclaimed your life, liberated yourself from toxicity, and redefined what relationships mean to you. You are not defined by your past; you are defined by the boundless potential of your future. With each step you take, may your journey be filled with love, self-acceptance, and authentic connections. Your story is still being written, and it is one of empowerment, healing, and the triumph of the human spirit.

Appendix: Additional Resources

This appendix provides a list of additional resources to support you on your journey of breaking free from toxic relationships, healing, and personal growth.

1. Books:

- "Why Does He Do That? Inside the Minds of Angry and Controlling Men" by Lundy Bancroft
- "The Verbally Abusive Relationship: How to Recognize It and How to Respond" by Patricia Evans
- "Codependent No More: How to Stop Controlling Others and Start Caring for Yourself" by Melody Beattie
- "The Power of Now: A Guide to Spiritual Enlightenment" by Eckhart Tolle
- "The Courage to Heal: A Guide for Women Survivors of Child Sexual Abuse" by Ellen Bass and Laura Davis

2. Support Groups:

- National Domestic Violence Hotline (USA): Call 1-800-799-SAFE (7233) or visit www.thehotline.org[1] for support and resources.
- Narcotics Anonymous (NA): www.na.org[2]
- Al-Anon Family Groups: www.al-anon.org[3]
- CoDA (Co-Dependents Anonymous): www.coda.org[4]

3. Online Communities:

---

1. http://www.thehotline.org/

2. http://www.na.org/

3. http://www.al-anon.org/

4. http://www.coda.org/

- Reddit: Subreddits such as r/relationship_advice, r/survivorsofabuse, and r/NarcissisticAbuse offer supportive communities where you can share experiences and seek advice.

4. Therapy and Counseling:

- Consider seeking therapy or counseling from licensed professionals who specialize in trauma, abuse, or relationship issues. Psychology Today's therapist directory (www.psychologytoday.com[5]) is a helpful resource for finding therapists in your area.

5. Legal Resources:

- Consult with an attorney for legal advice regarding divorce, custody, restraining orders, or any legal matters related to your situation.

6. Crisis Hotlines:

- If you are in immediate danger or crisis, please call your local emergency number or a crisis hotline. In the United States, you can call 911.

7. Apps:

- There are various mental health and self-help apps available that can assist with managing stress, anxiety, and other emotional challenges. Examples include BetterHelp, Talkspace, and Calm.

8. Workshops and Seminars:

- Many organizations offer workshops and seminars on personal

---

5. http://www.psychologytoday.com/

development, self-esteem, and healing from trauma. Check local community centers or online platforms for options in your area.

9. Podcasts:

- Podcasts like "The Love, Happiness and Success Podcast" by Dr. Lisa Marie Bobby and "The Overwhelmed Brain" by Paul Colaianni can provide valuable insights and advice on relationships and personal growth.

10. Crisis Centers: - Local crisis centers may offer immediate assistance, counseling, and shelter for individuals in abusive situations. Search online for crisis centers in your area.

Remember that seeking help and support is a sign of strength, and you do not have to face these challenges alone. These resources are here to assist you on your path to healing, growth, and the pursuit of healthy, fulfilling relationships.

Milton Keynes UK
Ingram Content Group UK Ltd.
UKHW010248221123
432980UK00005B/484